SO YOU WANT TO
WRITE A BOOK

OS HILLMAN

SO YOU WANT TO
WRITE A BOOK

How to Write, Publish and Market Your Book

Aslan Group Publishing
PO Box 69
Cumming, Georgia 30028 USA
678.455.6262
www.marketplaceleaders.org

ISBN: 978-1-888582-25-3

Contents

one

How I Started Writing

I'll never forget when God revealed to me that writing was going to be a part of my future. I was at a conference when a woman who was known for her prophetic gift passed me in the hallway. She stopped me and said, "Os, I don't know what God is doing with you, but when I see you I see the letters W-R-I-T-E over your head. You are going to write many books.

I was going through a season of great adversity at the time in the mid 90s. God was birthing something new in my life through that adversity. I could not make sense of that word at the time.

It would be a few years later when I did begin writing *TGIF Today God Is First* devotional. God would give me a scripture verse each day for nine months and the application to what I was going through. I began sharing these messages with friends on my email list. This went on for months. There were a few days when I failed to send out the devotional message. I got emails from people saying, "Where is my devotional?"

That was the first indication that these messages were helping people. Once I completed all of the 365 messages many encouraged me to put them in a book. I began to make contact with Christian publishers. I thought it would be an easy thing to do since I had worked with many Christian publishers through my ad agency. However, it was not as easy as I thought it would be. I became increasingly frustrated. I thought, "Maybe I need to self-publish this book," I said to a close friend.

My friend turned to me and said very forcefully," When you finish writing the book God will give you a publisher!"

I wasn't quite finished with the book at the time she said those words to me. A strange thing happened on the day that I finished writing number three hundred and sixty-five of the messages. I had an appointment that day in my city with a Christian publisher who happened to be in town. He had taken an interest in what I was doing. By the end of that day the publisher made me an offer for a publishing contract on my devotional book.

Turns out, my friend was prophetic. When I finished writing the book the publisher came into my path.

I started writing the devotional not thinking about whether it would ever be published. I was primarily writing for me. I was trying to make sense of the season of adversity I was walking through. It was really a form of Bible study and seeking answers for myself.

Sometimes God calls you to write but you may not know the reason for the writing. You might be writing for yourself or you might be writing for others. What you write might get published and it might not. The important thing is, if God calls you to write then you are simply to obey and start writing. You must leave the outcome to God.

My devotional began to get circulated through the internet. A friend of mine ran a major Christian internet website. He asked if he could put the devotional on his website and send out the messages for me. When that happened I began to hear from people from all over the world. People from other nations began writing me and telling me how much these devotionals were impacting their life.

I was still in a very difficult place in my life. Finances were very tight. English was not a subject that I excelled in school. I made average grades and my grammar skills were weak. I would often have people write me and say, "I love your devotional, but have you ever thought about having someone look at your work before you send it out? There are often many grammatical errors in your messages."

At that point I had to decide what to do about those comments. I could not afford to hire an editor. So, I decided it would be better for me to obey instead of worry about a few comments that came back every so often.

One day I got one of these email messages from a man in Hong He suggested that I get an editor to look at my work. I said to him, "How about you?"

He responded by offering to be my long distance editor. He was an English teacher in Hong Kong. So God provided an editor for me from Hong Kong—for free!

That is yet another lesson I learned in the process. Was I willing to risk the embarrassment of not having perfect grammar at the expense of not writing what was on my heart? If you will obey God and do what you feel you're supposed to do He will provide what you need at the time that you need it. Obey what God is saying to you.

Writer versus Author

I have a golfing buddy who was the senior editor at a major Christian publishing company. He worked for the largest Christian publisher in the world and was the senior editor for some top authors. I'll never forget something he said to me that gave me great peace and confidence to move forward in writing. He said to me, "Os, there are authors and there are writers. You are an author. You have something to say, but you may not have the skill set to write technically correct. That is why you need an editor. There are many who have important things to say but need a trained writer to help them communicate it in the form of a book.

A writer can write about any subject. They are trained in the art of writing and they enjoy writing about any subject. My friend said, "Os, you are called to write only about your experiences and what God is giving you to write about. You are an author, not a technical writer."

There are many freelance editors around. If you need an editor, call a local newspaper, online magazine or Christian publisher for referrals. Also, there are online options. Outsource.com can provide an editor for your project in a matter of minutes.

You should know that less than 1% of authors actually earn a living from the books they write and sell.

God Will Lead You

Proverbs 3:5,6 says "Trust in the Lord with all your heart, lean not on your own understanding; Acknowledge Him in all thy ways and He shall direct thy paths." I have learned that whatever God has called you to do, He will guide you in the fulfillment of that calling. Our role is to respond to His leading through obedience. Obedience starts with obeying the small things.

Family Christian Bookstores

Shortly after I published my first book I got an email from someone who worked as a buyer for Family Christian Bookstores, the largest Christian bookstore chain in America. I called the man and he shared with me how much TGIF had impacted his life. He wondered if I would be interested in providing three 100-page books on a topic of my interest that they could brand as a Family Christian title, but make it available to me after the print run of 5,000 ran out. Wow! I could not believe it! Here was the largest Christian bookstore chain in America asking me to write three books for them. I wrote the three titles and these three titles became part of our resources for our ministry.

A few years later I had about six books in publication. I was beginning to sense I needed a publishing partner who would work with me on a long-term basis. Shortly after that I was at a conference and ran into an old publishing client from my ad agency days. This client was a large Christian publishing company. They learned about what I was doing and they had just launched a new division in their company. They said, "Come see us. We are interested in what you are doing."

A few weeks later we met and they offered me a book contract. However, there were some things in the contract I could not agree with and they refused to remove the requirement from their contract. I let the contract go. It was a death of a vision for me. I was saddened and felt a lost opportunity had taken place. But I knew I made the right decision.

One day several months later I was in my office working. A book and letter arrived from a publisher. It was announcing a book by my friend Peter Wagner. The letter was from the president of Regal Books out of California. This company represented several people I knew and their authors were consistent with my theology. I said to myself, "Now this is a company that I should partner with."

The next morning I was at my desk and began a letter to the president. However, within a few minutes I felt a strange check in my spirit. I began to write, but then could not write. I had a sense I was not to write this letter. So, I stopped.

The next day I did the same thing. I started the letter only to feel I was hearing, "Don't write this letter." It was a strange experience. Nevertheless, I stopped writing the letter and concluded, for whatever reason, the Lord did not want me to pursue this company.

A few months later I was speaking at the headquarters of Peter Wagner's Prayer Center in Colorado Springs. I was teaching an all day workshop. Peter asked me to join him for lunch. When I walked into the room a man was sitting there with Peter. He introduced himself as Bill, the president of Regal Books. We had not been in the room more than 10 minutes when he turned to me and said these words: "We've been watching you for several years. We would love to publish anything you would like to write. We would like to be your publishing partner."

I nearly fell out of my chair! Immediately the Holy Spirit brought back to my mind the day I tried to write the letter to this very man. This was why I was not supposed to write the letter. God was going to personally arrange a meeting and prompt the publisher to invite me to publish with them. In business it is always better if a business partner pursues you than if you pursue the partner. It changes the relationship when the business partner desires to be in business with you instead of you trying to sell them on yourself. You are operating from a stronger position as the one being pursued. I entered a publishing relationship with this company and published 3 books with them over a 7-year period.

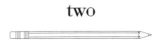

two

How Publishing Has Changed in the Last Few Decades

There was a time when an author could have an important message presented to a publisher and the publisher would consider the book based on the merits of the message. That is not so today. Today, to have a book project considered by a publisher you must not only have a good message, but you must also have a broad enough audience who a publisher believes will buy the book and the author must have an already established audience. In many cases, the publisher will require the author to buy 1,000-5,000 copies before they will even consider your project.

This is not true of celebrity authors. A celebrity author is one who has a television show or is a well-known personality that has a following. Publishers are willing to take less and less risk today on new authors. The only thing that justifies a publisher publishing your book is the expectation that enough people will buy the book and show a profit.

The Writing Process

Start collecting ideas for your book and future books. I am always on the lookout for new ideas. I make a note section on my iPhone to jot down ideas on a particular issue or subject I might want to write about in the future. Some of these ideas will be topics for new books, future articles or chapters in a new book. Many times God will give me an expanded understanding of a concept others initially introduced.

Determine the word count of your book

In the digital age the attention span of American readers is getting shorter and shorter. Some works of fiction by skillful writers are an exception to this. But in the non-fiction Christian market, books are getting shorter. The standard size non-fiction paperback book is 6" by 9" and averages 200 pages. The industry average for nonfiction is around 300 words per page. So that is 60,000 words in total. There is a trend going from books of 60,000-70,000 words to word counts of 20,000 to 45,000 words. If you are a new writer, be careful with the number of words you write. Beginning writers almost always write too much. These could mean two or three books instead of one. Big does not always mean better. Some of the greatest best sellers have been small digest books under 150 pages. Keep track of your word counts by chapter to know where you are in the process. Using an excel spreadsheet with each chapter and word count is an easy way to do this.

Standalone Chapters

Go back to your outline and assign a certain number of words for each chapter which total the number of words you desire in the whole book. Then do the same, if possible, for your chapter sub-headings. Make a spreadsheet to make it simple. Make each chapter a separate document on your computer so you can constantly check up on your word count. If you discipline yourself in this process you will save a lot of time and frustration. The writing will be much more manageable because you will only have to write 300, 500 or 1000 words on a given subject. The preparation takes time, but it is time well invested so try not to take short cuts. This also allows you to make each chapter available as a promotional tool should you choose to do so. Today you can set up websites just for your book. It is good to have two or three chapters available free on these sites.

Go into a Book-writing Mode

When I start a project I am very focused and disciplined every day to write. Block out time stealers and be careful how many outside distractions come in during this time. I mentioned earlier that my writing time is 5-10 AM. After that I find I am not as creative or productive.

Write Chapter by Chapter in Order

It is important to remember what you have said to avoid being redundant. Sometimes making an outline with all the stories helps avoid duplication. Chapters should flow from one to the next. When you begin a new chapter, go over your sub-points because you might want to change them at some point.

Subtitles

Subtitles make reading your material easier. It also helps potential readers become familiar with what you are writing about by just flipping through the pages of your book. Some will decide to purchase your book just by looking at a subtitle or two that strikes their interest.

Edit as you go Along

Don't save your editing until the last. I always edit what I have written the day before I add new material. When you finish a chapter, edit that chapter and rewrite as much as you need to. Be careful about depending on spell-check to catch misspellings. It will not catch some words. You must read every word to check spelling. Each chapter should be considered a finished product. It is still necessary to final edit your whole book before completion, but this makes the final edit much easier. Always have someone else edit your work so you have fresh eyes looking at the material. They will catch things that you will often overlook.

There are no Perfect Books

There are two schools of thought about releasing books. One demands that every avenue of research and double-checking be exhausted before the book is published. No mistakes allowed. The other is to write what you know at the moment and get the ideas out there. If it turns out that you have made a mistake or that you subsequently change your opinion about something, no problem. Correct it in your next book!

Hardback versus Paperback

The only reason publishers publish hardbacks is to make more money. They can charge more for a hardback than a paperback. Many times a publisher will release a book in hardback and then release the paperback edition the following year.

Another consideration is to consider what type of book it is. I have written a number of devotional books. Two of these books have leather-like covers designed to create a warm, and long-lasting feel. Devotionals are used everyday and need to have a binding that will last. Using a cover that is soft to the feel contributes to the overall devotional experience for the reader.

three

Understanding eBook Publishing, Distribution & Marketing Fees

The internet has changed publishing. Whereas it used to be cost prohibitive to self-publish a book, digital printing has changed all of that. A book can be designed and printed in quantities as little as 50, 100 or 200 copies at a reasonable price of $2-$5 per unit. There is now an entire industry catering to the self-publishing market. I have listed some of these sources at the end of this book. The trade-off is that the look of your book can be unprofessional if you don't have a professional designer design your cover. If you self-publish and market your own book you must invest the capital necessary to publish it. The cost of this has come down incredibly, but you will need some funds to print. If you only create an ebook, then you can virtually publish for nothing. Discerning readers often have a lower regard for a self-published book if they perceive it is not done with excellence, referring to it as "vanity press." However, this is changing due to the volume of self-published books on the market today and the professionalism being exhibited through the websites who specialize in self-publishing.

Create Space

Amazon has a program called Create Space that is the self-publishing arm of Amazon. They provide soup-to-nuts publishing from cover design, to layout, to printing and distribution. This is a great solution as you will automatically have the huge distribution of Amazon at your disposal. You can purchase copies for your use and their print-on-demand feature keeps your inventory low and your price point at a level where you can still make money on your title. Learn more at: www.createspace.com

eBooks

eBooks have changed publishing. No longer do you even have to publish a printed book. You can literally finish your book and have it selling on Amazon or Barnes and Noble or Apple's iBooks in twenty-four hours. There are companies that specialize in preparing your eBook and selling it to all the major outlets that sell eBooks. One such group is Inscribe. They specialize in formatting and marketing your eBook title. All ebooks must be formatted correctly to be able to be read in ebook readers like tablets, Nooks, etc.

Inscribe Digital.com

INscribe Digital helps you manage your book by providing you with a streamlined process from original file to retail delivery. As global eBook distributors, their expertise allows you to produce eBooks that will pass all retailer requirements.

Their website describes their services:
- Conversion of your title from any source file, including XML, HTML, Word, PDF, InDesign, and Quark.
- Scanning and OCR of print books, microfilm, application files, and more.
- Print-ready PDFs for your print on demand or off-set printing needs.
- Competitive pricing, free quotes, and price comparisons.
- Rush conversions in 2-3 days.*
- File repairs, upgrades, and quality assurance for your existing eBook files.
- Read-along options for children's books.
- EPUB 2.0, EPUB 3.0, and MOBI.
- Enhanced eBooks with video, audio, or read-along.
- Interactive iBooks files.
- Social media add-ons.
- The provide custom development as well.
- ISBN number: Inscribe can provide ISBN numbers for $10.

What it Costs

Inscribe markets titles to major retailers of ebooks. Here is the list of on-line retailers and the percentage of the retail price they pay to the client. (check current pricing)

Pricing Your eBook

Ideal price for an ebook is $2.99 to 9.99, but it needs to stay under 9.99 to get 70% margin with Amazon KDP or it will drop to 35% if it is over $9.99

Payments: You will receive monthly electronic payments via ACP or paypal, a minimum $100 , $250 for checks.

Amazon Kindle

Following is the Amazon Kindle Direct Publishing KDP Commission Structure
- If product retails $2.99 - $9.99 the rate is 70% to client
- If product retails below $2.99 or above $9.99 35% goes to client

Should You License Your Book with a Publisher?

There are advantages and disadvantages of going with a publisher to sell your book. The two biggest advantages are 1) retail distribution, and 2) recognition and validation.

Publishers represent your book to wholesale distributors who sell to bookstores, Amazon, and mass retail marketers like Walmart. They have a formula they follow as it relates to selling books to retailers. They are going to have to sell your $15- 20 hardcover or softcover book for 60-70% off retail, or $8-9. They will sell your book to distributors who then sell to retail stores for 40-50% discount. You are paid a royalty off that net sale price. So, if you make a 15% royalty on every sale, you will get $1.20 for each book that sells for $8. There is also a return policy that is required from major retailers.

You will be allowed to purchase books for yourself at 60-80% off re-tailer depending on the quantity you buy and you will not be paid a royalty on those book purchases. Royalty amounts are often set on a graduated scale based on the number of books sold. It can go from 10-25%.

There is usually an advance paid to an author from a major publisher. This figure is based on how may books the publisher thinks they can sell. This figure can range $7,500 to $10,000 or more depending on the author's name recognition in the market. There are some publishers who do not pay advance royalties, especially if you are a first-time author.

Co-Publishing

Another option to consider is co-publishing. In co-publishing an established publishing house agrees to publish your manuscript providing you place a pre-publication order of a certain number of copies. Although there is no assurance beforehand that the publisher will accept your manuscript, the chances that they will are higher because they know they will sell enough copies (to you) to pay their bills. Your book will have a professional look, and the publisher will handle ISBN numbers, copyrights, cover design and editing. Currently Creation House Press is serving authors with co-publishing agreements. Keep in mind that you will need up-front capital; you will do most of the marketing of your book except to retail stores which is the primary benefit of co-publishing.

Recognition and Validation

The second reason you might want to publish with a publisher is the recognition and validation you receive from being published by a publisher. There is a perception by some that if you are not published by a publisher, then you are not a legitimate author. This is starting to change the more people become successful in the self-publishing arena. I have also seen where some who started with a publisher opted to self-publish later because they felt they could sell more books than the publisher. I have chosen to do that with some of my books. I have been published by four major publishers over my publishing career. I have published about 60% of my titles with major publishers and self-published the others.

Another consideration is that it is going to take 9-12 months to get your book out from the time you sign a contract with a publisher. If you self-publish, you can be on the street in 30-60 days. There will also be a more stringent editorial process that may make you feel you are losing control of your content if you are not careful. However, in most cases, the editorial team will make your product better.

Another rule of thumb for me is that I will work with a major publisher if my title is a major book I want to achieve broad retail distribution. If I write a 100-page book that is more topical or is a teaching resource, I will always self-publish that title. Publishers won't publish such a small book usually.

If a book does not take off in the first 3-6 months, you will most likely see your book backlisted and it will be treated as simply a book in inventory, but they will not invest promotional dollars into the title any more. I was once told by the marketing director of a major publisher that they would not put money in advertising my book unless it achieved a certain level of sales in the first few months. I was furious. I responded by saying, "Advertising is the water that goes into the pump to create sales! Your logic is backwards!" I was very upset with their reasoning. The next time I publish with that publisher there will be a guaranteed amount for advertising and public relations built into the contract or I will not publish with them.

When to Write – Avoiding Procrastination

"All hard work brings a profit, but mere talk leads only to poverty"
—Proverbs 14:23

One of the questions I am often asked is what is the process I use to write a book and when do I write it? I mentioned earlier that I am a morning person. I get up around 5am and go to bed around 10pm. I have learned over the years my most creative time is between 5am-8am. I find that I am often too concerned with other activities after that time. So, if I am writing a book, that is the time I devote to writing every day.

How I write a book depends on the type of book it is going to be. Usually I have a rough outline of what the contents will cover. I do all my own research. Some books require more research while others are written from personal experience. It is important to understand who you are writing to. Knowing your audience is important to be able to write to them.

Many times people tell me they believe they are called to write a book. I tell them, "Great, if God has called you to write a book, then start writing it." Sometimes the response is: "But I don't have time, or I don't have a publisher."

"That has nothing to do with it," I say.

That is not your problem. If God calls you to write a book, you are to begin to write it. You may not be writing to get published. You may be writing for other purposes. You could even be writing it for yourself. When I first began writing *TGIF Today God Is First*, I was really writing as a means of processing what God was doing in my own life. It was later I felt I was to share it with others.

If God has given you a vision to write, begin by taking baby steps toward that project. You might only write twenty-five words a day. But, in 100 days you will have written 2500 words. Begin to focus on the vision and take action steps toward it.

Many times people ask me, "How in the world do you have time to write? You travel so much and seem to have such a full schedule." You will be amazed at what God can do with a little each day. Do not let procrastination prevent you from accomplishing what God may want to do through your life. Make plans today to take baby steps toward the book that is in your heart.

Type or Dictate?

We live in a wonderful technology age. What we can do today boggles my mind. I am old enough to remember writing some of my books on a typewriter. Later I had a black and white apple computer. OK, I am showing my age.

I am so thankful for the 7th grade beginner typing class I was required to take. It is one skill I have kept from those grade school years. However, the good news for those of you who are not great typists is that you no longer need to type to write a book. I literally wrote one small book on the note section of my iPhone by dictating to it. The dictation apps available on your computer, smart phone or iPad are great resources today. Dragon is a dictation software many have used. However, most smartphones have this feature built in to their software. Dragon is a free app/software for your smart phone, ipad or computer. You dictate to your phone or computer and it translates it into text. Then, all you have to do is edit what you dictate. It is a great way to write a book. I find it is also helpful to dictate because you process your words slower than typing.

You need to decide your best way of communicating and getting words on paper.

I was told several years ago that the average book is written at a twelve-year old reading level. Avoid words that might not be easily understood by a twelve-year old. Unfortunately, our society is becoming less literate and people read less and will not invest time in lengthy books.

Audio books have become popular for busy people who spend time in their car. I have recorded several of my books as audio books. Two main resources for distributing audio books are AudioBooks.com and Audible.com.

four

Layout, Design, Printing and Permission Rules

If you decide to self-publish your book, you will need to get an ISBN # for your title. The ISBN number is what publishing uses to track every book title. There is a unique ISBN number for each version of your title – hardback, paperback, and eBook. R.R. Bowker and Company is the source to acquire your ISBN #. It is very inexpensive to acquire your number and this can be done in 24 hours (See website details in Addendum).

Permission Guidelines

In some situations, you may make limited use of another's copyrighted work without asking permission or infringing on the original copyright. The following has been excerpted from a website that gives you all you need to know about gaining permissions for quoting others in your work.

Sooner or later, almost all writers quote or closely paraphrase what others have written. For example:

- Andy, putting together a newsletter on his home computer, reprints an editorial he likes from a daily newspaper.
- Phil, a biographer and historian, quotes from several unpublished letters and diaries written by his subject.
- Regina, a freelance writer, closely paraphrases two paragraphs from the Encyclopedia Britannica in an article she's writing.
- Sylvia, a poet, quotes a line from a poem by T.S. Eliot in one of her own poems.
- Donnie, a comedian, writes a parody of the famous song "Blue Moon" he performs in his comedy act.

Assuming the material quoted in these examples is protected by copyright, do Phil, Regina, Sylvia, Andy, and Donnie need permission from the author or other copyright owner to use it? It may surprise you to learn that the answer is "not necessarily."

Under the "fair use" rule of copyright law, an author may make limited use of another author's work without asking permission. Fair use is based on the belief that the public is entitled to freely use portions of copyrighted materials for purposes of commentary and criticism. The fair use privilege is perhaps the most significant limitation on a copyright owner's exclusive rights. If you write or publish, you need a basic understanding of what is and is not fair use.

Uses That Are Generally Fair Uses

Subject to some general limitations discussed later in this article, the following types of uses are usually deemed fair uses:

Criticism and comment— for example, quoting or excerpting a work in a review or criticism for purposes of illustration or comment.

News reporting— for example, summarizing an address or article, with brief quotations, in a news report.

Research and scholarship— for example, quoting a short passage in a scholarly, scientific, or technical work for illustration or clarification of the author's observations.

Nonprofit educational uses— for example, photocopying of limited portions of written works by teachers for classroom use.

Parody— that is, a work that ridicules another, usually well-known, work by imitating it in a comic way.

In most other situations, copying is not legally a fair use. Without an author's permission, such a use violates the author's copyright.

Non-commercial use is often fair use. Violations often occur when the use is motivated primarily by a desire for commercial gain. The fact that a work is published primarily for private commercial gain weighs against a finding of fair use. For example, using the Bob Dylan line "You don't need a weatherman to know which way the wind blows" in a poem published in a small literary journal would probably be a fair use; using the same line in an advertisement for raincoats probably would not be.

Benefit to the public may be fair use. A commercial motive doesn't always disqualify someone from claiming a fair use. A use that benefits the public can qualify as a fair use, even if it makes money for the user.

For example, in its advertising a vacuum cleaner manufacturer was permitted to quote from a *Consumer Reports* article comparing vacuum cleaners. Why? The ad significantly increased the number of people exposed to the Consumers Reports' evaluations and thereby disseminated helpful consumer information. The same rationale probably applies to the widespread practice of quoting from favorable reviews in advertisements for books, films, and plays.

When Is a Use a "Fair Use"?

There are five basic rules to keep in mind when deciding whether or not a particular use of an author's work is a fair use:

Rule 1: Are You Creating Something New or Just Copying?

The purpose and character of your intended use of the material involved is the single most important factor in determining whether a use is a fair use. The question to ask here is whether you are merely copying someone else's work verbatim or instead using it to help create something new.

Rule 2: Are You Competing with the Source You're Copying From?

Without consent, you ordinarily cannot use another person's protected expression in a way that impairs (or even potentially impairs) the market for his or her work.

For example, say Nick, a golf pro, writes a book on how to play golf. He copies several brilliant paragraphs on putting from a book by Lee Trevino, one of the greatest putters in golf history. Because Nick intends his book to compete with and hopefully supplant Trevino's, this use is not a fair use.

Rule 3: Giving the Author Credit Doesn't Let You Off the Hook

Some people mistakenly believe that they can use any material as long as they properly give the author credit. Not true. Giving credit and fair use are completely separate concepts. Either you have the right to use another author's material under the fair use rule or you don't. The fact that you attribute the material to the other author doesn't change that.

Rule 4: The More You Take, the Less Fair Your Use Is Likely to Be

The more material you take, the less likely it is that your use will be a fair use. As a general rule, never: quote more than a few successive paragraphs from a book or article, take more than one chart or diagram, include an illustration or other artwork in a book or newsletter without the artist's permission, or quote more than one or two lines from a poem.

Contrary to what many people believe, there is no absolute word limit on fair use. For example, copying 200 words from a work of 300 words wouldn't be fair use. However, copying 2000 words from a work of 500,000 words might be fair. It all depends on the circumstances.

To preserve the free flow of information, authors have more leeway in using material from factual works (scholarly, technical, and scientific works) than to works of fancy such as novels, poems, and plays.

Rule 5: The Quality of the Material Used Is as Important as the Quantity

The more important the material is to the original work, the less likely your use of it will be considered a fair use.

In one famous case, *The Nation* magazine obtained a copy of Gerald Ford's memoirs before their publication. In the magazine's article about the memoirs, only 300 words from Ford's 200,000-word manuscript were quoted verbatim. The Supreme Court ruled that this was not a fair use because the material quoted (dealing with the Nixon pardon) was the "heart of the book ... the most interesting and moving parts of the entire manuscript," and that pre-publication disclosure of this material would cut into value or sales of the book.

In determining whether your intended use of another author's protected work constitutes a fair use the golden rule: Take from someone else only what you wouldn't mind someone taking from you.

Copying from Unpublished Materials

When it comes to fair use, unpublished works are inherently different from published works. Publishing an author's unpublished work before he or she has authorized it infringes upon the author's right to decide when and whether the work will be made public.

Some courts in the past held that fair use never applies to unpublished material. However, in 1991 Congress amended the fair use provision in the Copyright Act to make clear that the fact that a work is unpublished weighs against fair use, but is not determinative in and of itself.

For more detailed information on fair use and copyrighted material, see *Getting Permission: How to License & Clear Copyrighted Materials Online & Off*, by Richard Stim (Nolo).

Should you copyright your work?

When you've created something original, such as a book, you want to ensure that your work—whether published or unpublished—is protected. Copyrighting your work through common law is a way of proving that the work is your own, but official registration is necessary before you have any power to take action against someone who is stealing or profiting from your work.

Know the law for your location. If your country is a signatory to the Berne Convention for the Protection of Literary and Artistic Works—and that covers most countries in the world—then your work is protected from the moment you create it in a format that is "perceptible either directly or with the aid of a machine or device."

That means that you automatically own the copyright to any original work you create—as long as you commit it to readable form. For the current list of countries that are signatories to the Berne Convention, visit the World Intellectual Property Organization (WIPO) at http://www.wipo.int/members/en/

WIPO does not offer a registration service for copyright, but it does acknowledge that many countries have national registration systems in place and that for some countries, this serves as prima facie evidence in a court of law as to copyright ownership. You will want to display your copyright in the first few pages before your table of contents listed as follows: Copyright © 2015 your name

Following is a link to how to apply for copyright.

www.copyright.gov

International Rights

Whenever you are represented by a publisher they handle international rights. That means that they will pitch your book to publishers in other countries for publishing in that country. The typical income split is 50% of the proceeds from these sources.

There is one group I am aware of that handles international representation for Christian titles that currently represent my titles. Gospel Literature International will represent your titles to international publishers. Their fee for representation is 25% of the net received from the international publisher.

Gospel Literature International (GLINT)

2980 Inland Empire Blvd., Suite 102

Ontario, California 91764 USA

Phone: 909.481-5222 - Fax: 909.481-5216

Website: www.glint.org

five

Marketing Your Book

Now that you have published your book you need people to buy it. If you are a lone author who is self-publishing your book, then you must find ways of getting your book noticed and purchased.

Website— It should go without saying that you need a website where you can write and share about your topic and provide links to purchasing your book.

Amazon.com has become the primary source where books are bought online today. CreateSpace.com is the self-publishing division that can take your book from text to finished product and help you market your book.

Public Relations— There are public relations agencies who can be hired to place you on radio stations or TV programs to talk about your book.

Blog— Start a blog and use content from the book and links to purchase the book. As your blog audience grows it is the best place to share about your book.

Online Stores— Contact other online stores to get your book carried by them. Barnes & Noble is another source.

Social Media— Facebook, Twitter, LinkedIN, and Instagram are key to building an audience where you can share about your book.

Workshops— Another way to build an audience is to speak publicly about your topic. Begin to teach workshops on the topic of your book. Become an authority on your subject.

Guest Editorials— Start writing for online media. I am a regular contributor to Christian online media. This is a great source to build an audience.

eBook Marketing— Smashwords.com is a source for marketing your ebook. https://www.smashwords.com

GoodReads.com is a gathering place for authors who want to feature their work and help promote it to a large book reading audience. Here is what they say about themselves: Gain access to a massive audience of more than 40 million book lovers. GoodReads.com is a great place to promote your books.

Developing Your Customer Base Using ARTT

Several years ago I became aware of a helpful process designed to help ministries and even businesses grow their customer base. It is called ARTT and stands for:

Acquaintance
Relationship
Trust
Transaction

Acquaintance

Here is how it works. In order to gain a new customer, member to your organization, or donor, it requires an intentional 4-phase process that takes an initial contact to a transaction. The first phase is called Acquaintance. This involves a strategy to develop an initial relationship with a potential prospect. Some typical ways your prospect might be introduced to your organization might be:

- Referral from a friend
- Outreach luncheon
- Article in a publication or broadcast media
- Trade show
- Conference
- Business associate referral
- Newsletter
- Business seminar
- Breakfast meeting

These are just a few of the ways people might come in contact with your organization. During this phase it is important not to do things that are more appropriate for the other three phases. For instance, in the Acquaintance stage you don't:

- Ask for an order
- Ask for money
- Introduce deeper spiritual concepts that non-believers might find a barrier to continuing the relationship. This is especially true for evangelistic ministries. So often we try to appeal to non-believers using religious jargon and introduce more mature spiritual concepts before they are ready to receive. It's like trying to feed steak to a newborn baby. They choke on it! And, you lose the relationship in the process.

Relationship

The second phase is Relationship. During this phase you are trying to go from a first acquaintance to an actual relationship. Your prospect gets to know you, what you stand for and whether they want to continue in the relationship. You build relationship by providing services to them with no strings attached. It is the courtship period. Again, you want to avoid deeper spiritual concepts if you are an evangelistic ministry until there is Trust relationship in place.

Trust

Trust is the third phase in the process. During this phase your prospect is learning to trust you. A formal engagement period has been initiated and they are deciding if they want to proceed to the fourth stage. Once you've established trust you are able to move to the Transaction phase.

Transaction

Transaction is the phase in which you have an actual transaction with your prospect. The transaction phase is different based upon the type of service or product you provide.

Transactions may include:

- Membership
- A product purchase
- Attendance to a conference
- A donation
- Openness to deeper spiritual concepts
- Book purchase
- Getting a speaking engagement

Whenever you try to gain a transaction in phase 1, 2, or 3 you risk the loss of the prospective customer. It's like trying to kiss your blind date before you've even spoken to them. It just doesn't work. You are violating the relationship when you do this.

It's Your Turn

Take a few minutes and list the various ways you make a first acquaintance through your organization in the space below.

Next, list the things you are currently doing in phase 1, 2, or 3 that should be reserved for phase 4.

_____

_____

_____

_____

_____

_____

_____

_____

_____

Describe new things you can do in phase l designed to generate new acquaintances.

_____

_____

_____

_____

_____

_____

_____

_____

Do the same for phase 2 and 3.

_____

_____

_____

_____

_____

_____

_____

_____

_____

Following these steps will allow you to grow a loyal customer, member or donor.

A final thought

The internet is a great place to find new ways of marketing your book. I encourage you to spend time on the internet researching book selling opportunities. Like technology, it is hard to keep up with all the latest trends in book marketing. Now, what are you waiting on? Start writing that book!

Helpful Resources

Publishing Proposal Outline

Following is a sample proposal outline from a major publisher. This is an excellent tool to help you think through the content and audience and message of your book.

Author:

Working Title:

Proposed Subtitle:

Agent?:

Premise: (Provide a two- or three-sentence statement of the book's central concept. Often this is worded as a problem and the solution the book provides.)

Benefits: After completing (title), readers will: (List the benefits or take-away value readers will derive from the book.)

Features: (Explain how the book will deliver the benefits by listing the book's unique features.)

Overview: The book is divided into (number) sections and (number) chapters.

The Manuscript

Manuscript Status: (State how much of the manuscript is complete)

Anticipated Word Count: (280 words per page)

Anticipated Manuscript Completion Date:

Description: (Summarize the principal message or concepts of your book. Use language that is concrete and specific. Think in terms of what you want the reader to understand and apply to his or her life.)

- 30 words or less:

- 100 words or less:

- 250 words or less:

The Market

Characteristics: The target audience for this book is made up of... (Describe the demographic characteristics of the target readers, including age, sex, education level, etc.)

Motivations: (Describe the psychographic characteristics of the target readers, including the frustrations, desires, etc., that would motivate them to purchase and read the book.)

Affinity Groups: (List the groups of people, organizations, etc., who are likely to be attracted to the book.)

Differentiation: (Describe the main competition for the book and explain what distinguishes this book from them.)

The Author

Background: (Give a brief biographical description making sure to include information that establishes your credibility or qualifications to the write the book.)

Previous Writing: (List previously published writing, including the name of the publisher, the date of publication, the number of units sold, current status of each book.)

If the material/book being submitted for consideration has been self or previously published, please provide name of publishing house, year first published, year book went out of print and sales history (all that apply). Also, please indicate if rights have been returned to you.

Previously published by:

Year published:

Out of print:

Sales History:

Future Writing Ideas:

List of speaking engagements for the next twelve to eighteen months:

Possible Foreword writer/Endorsers: (List the names of people who are likely to provide a written endorsement of the book.)

Personal Marketing: (Describe what the you can do to help the publisher promote the book.)

Chapter Outline: (Provide an annotated outline of the book. This outline should include section titles, chapter titles, and a two- or three-sentence description of each chapter's content.)

Sample Chapters: (Attach two sample chapters that best represent the book.)

Publishing Resources

Acquiring your ISBN Number
R.R. Bowker
www.isbn-us.com

Book Printing Resources
Family Foundations International
www.familyfoundations.com
303.797.1139

Permission Guidelines
For more detailed information on fair use and copyrighted material,
see *Getting Permission: How to License & Clear Copyrighted Materials
Online & Off*, by Richard Stim (Nolo).
Source: *www.nolo.com*

Permission Guidelines for Authors
John Wiley and Sons Free PDF download
www.authorservices.wiley.com

Copyright Information
www.copyright.gov

International Rights
Gospel Literature International (GLINT)
2980 Inland Empire Blvd., Suite 102
Ontario, California 91764 USA
Phone: 909.481-5222 - Fax: 909.481-5216
www.glint.org

Self-publishing Resources
CreateSpace.com is a division of Amazon that allows you to create
and publish your own title. They allow you to print only what you need
and cover everything from getting an ISBN number to cover design to
finished printing and marketing through *Amazon.com*.

Westbow Press, division of Thomas Nelson is a co-publishing resource.
Free guide offered.
www.westbowpress.com

Xulon Press is another very popular co-publishing resource. Free guide offered.
www.XulonPress.com

Creation House Press is a Christian co-publishing resource that will do a modified publishing contract whereby you pay for the printing of your book and they will represent it to the retail market. They are a division of Charisma Media Publishing.
600 Rinehart Rd.
Lake Mary FL 32746
www.creationhouse.com

Smashwords Book Marketing
Mark Coker
www.smashwords.com

Inscribe ebook creators and marketers will represent your ebook to all the online book retailers.
www.inscribedigital.com

Outsource.com can help you find an editor for your project.
www.outsource.com

Graphic Design – I have had a long-term relationship with a designer named Ed Tuttle in Connecticut. Ed is the consummate professional and can help you design a great cover.
www.eklektos.com

Designcrowd.com - Today there are low cost avenues for graphic work as well. With Designcrowd.com you bid out your book cover design and choose the one you like best. You can even set your own price. I was amazed to get a well-designed book cover for only $180!

You can get brochures, logos, book covers – just about anything related to graphic design.
www.Designcrowd.com

Voices.com – Need to promote your book on radio or a simple audio promo? Voices.com allows you to bid out your voiceover project.
www.voices.com

Leadpages.net is a great source for creating landing pages and web pages without needing to know code for capturing names for marketing purposes. They also have a service to use your cell phone for text messaging a number and getting that lead sent to an email address. This is great for speakers who want to have immediate audience response to an offer.
www.leadpages.net

Book Trade Associations

These associations can provide a listing of book publishers. They can also identify book distributors for you.

American Book Association
www.bookweb.org

Christian Booksellers Association
www.cbaonline.org

Additional Resources by Os Hillman

Visit *www.MarketplaceLeaders.org* or *www.TGIFBookstore.com*

Receive TGIF Today God Is First and to stay connected to Os Hillman:

iPhone - TGIF iPhone App & Podcast through iTunes.com
www. marketplaceleaders.org/apps/

Email – *www.TodayGodIsFirst.com*

Facebook – *www.facebook.com/pages/TGIF-Today-God-Is-First*
Website – *www.TodayGodIsFirst.com*

Follow Os:

Twitter - *@oshillman*

LinkedIn – *Os Hillman*

Marketplace Community – *www.MLcommunity.com*

Change Agent Network – *www.BecomeaChangeAgent.net*

Other Books by Os Hillman

For additional resources from Os Hillman visit *www.tgifbookstore.com*

Listening to the Father's Heart devotional

Change Agent: How to be the one who makes a difference

Experiencing the Father's Love: How to live as sons and daughters of our Heavenly Father

The 9 To 5 Window: How Faith Can Transform The Workplace.

The Upside of Adversity: From the Pit to Greatness

TGIF Today God Is First, Volume 1 & 2

Making Godly Decisions

The Purposes of Money

Are You a Biblical Worker? Self-assessment

The Faith@Work Movement: What every pastor and church leader should know

TGIF Small Group Bible StudyFaith & Work: Do They Mix?

Proven Strategies for Business Success

Visit Our Websites

www.MarketplaceLeaders.org

www.Reclaim7Mountains.com

www.tgifbookstore.com

www.UpsideofAdversity.com

www.mlcommunity.com

www.becomeachangeagent.com

www.3GreatestLies.com

Marketplace Leaders
PO Box 69
Cumming, GA 30028
678.455.6262
info@marketplaceleaders.org
www.marketplaceleaders.org

About the Author

Os Hillman is president of Marketplace Leaders, an organization whose purpose is to help men and women discover and fulfill God's complete purposes through their work and to view their work as ministry.

Formally Os owned an advertising agency but is now an internationally recognized speaker on the subject of faith at work. He is the author of 15 books and a daily email devotional called *Today God Is First* that has several hundred thousand readers in 104 nations.

Os has been featured on *CNBC*, *NBC*, *LA Times*, *New York Times*, and many other national media as a spokesperson on faith at work. He is a regular contributor to *TwoTen magazine*, *ChristianPost.com*, *CharismaNews.com*, and *Crosswalk.com*.

Os is also president of Aslan, Inc. which provides a leading online "faith-at-work" Christian bookstore called *TGIFbookstore.com* to serve the needs of Christians in their workplace calling.

Os serves on the National Day of Prayer Committee. Os attended the University of South Carolina and Calvary Chapel Bible School, a ministry of Calvary Chapel of Costa Mesa, California.

50390879R00028

Made in the USA
Charleston, SC
28 December 2015